P9-BZI-653

Cascade Junior High School
Library

About the Book

Why is the sky blue when sunlight is white? Why do rainbows appear in the sky? Noted science author Melvin Berger explains the phenomenon of light in an illustrated, easy-to-understand format. Using simple diagrams to clarify difficult concepts, this book explores what light is and how we measure, record, perceive and use it. Also included are explanations of lenses, microscopes, telescopes, parts of the human eye, lasers and other light-related topics.

Lights, Lenses and Lasers

Melvin Berger

illustrations by Greg Wenzel

Cascade Junior High School
Library

G. P. Putnam's Sons • New York

Photo Credits
American Bank Note Company, pages 72, 73
Bell Laboratories, front cover, pages 48 (top left), 52, 53, 56
Better Vision Institute, pages 15, 28, 34, 36, 37, 38
Department of Energy, pages 66, 67
Hale Observatories, page 45
Harman/Kardon, page 70
Hughes Aircraft Company, pages 48 (bottom right), 51, 55, 60, 62, 64 (bottom left and top right)
International Business Machines Corporation, pages 59, 68
National Radio Astronomy Observatory, page 46
Yerkes Observatory, page 44

Copyright © 1987 by Melvin Berger
All rights reserved. Published simultaneously in Canada.
Printed in the United States of America
Book design by Martha Rago
Second impression

Library of Congress Cataloging-in-Publication Data
Berger, Melvin.   Lights, lenses and lasers.
Includes index. Summary: Examines the sources of
natural, artificial, biological, and reflected light
and the properties and uses of lenses and lasers.
1. Optical instruments—Juvenile literature.
2. Light sources—Juvenile literature. 3. Lenses—
Juvenile literature. 4. Lasers—Juvenile literature.
[1. Light. 2. Lenses. 3. Lasers. 4. Optics]
I. Wenzel, Gregory, ill. II. Title
QC371.4.B47 1987 535 87-10798
ISBN 0-399-61214-9

Contents

Introduction

Lights are all around you. There are many different sources of light—the sun, electric light bulbs, television screens, candles. And you can see different objects because they are struck by these lights—this book, the furniture in the room and the buildings, trees and cars outdoors.

Very often the light you see is bent or changed by passing through a glass or plastic lens. If you wear eyeglasses or contact lenses all the light reaching your eyes is seen through lenses. When you watch a movie or TV or look through a microscope or telescope, lenses have changed the images you see.

The laser ranks with the computer as one of the most astounding discoveries of 20th century science. This special, powerful form of light has, since its creation in 1960, found an amazing variety of uses—from destroying weapons in space to reading labels in supermarkets, from doing delicate surgery to communicating over vast distances.

Scientists already know a great deal about lights, lenses and lasers. And every day they learn even more about these truly fascinating subjects and how they can better serve mankind.

1.
Lights

Light, no matter where it comes from, spreads out in all directions like the spokes of a bicycle wheel. It travels invisibly and at enormous speed. Scientists consider light a form of energy. Like other forms of energy, light does work. It darkens film in a camera. It causes green plants to grow, through the process of photosynthesis. And light from the sun warms the earth and keeps us from freezing to death. Because it spreads out and does work, light is known as a form of *radiant energy*.

Natural Light

The sun is by far the most important source of radiant light energy. It provides almost all of our *natural light*.

The sun is always generating great amounts of energy. This closest of all stars is over 100 times the diameter of the earth. It is composed mostly of the element hydrogen, which is a gas. The heat and pressure within the huge ball of the sun are so tremendous that some of the hydrogen atoms are forced together. They combine to become larger atoms of the element helium. This process is called fusion. Man-made fusion is the basis of the superpowerful H-bomb (short for hydrogen bomb).

The fusion going on within the sun produces gigantic amounts of energy. Every second, day and night, nearly 800 million tons of hydrogen are fused into helium. It is like millions of gigantic H-bombs exploding all at once. This fusion releases a powerful flow of energy. Some of the energy is in the form of heat that we can feel. Some is in the form of visible light that we can see.

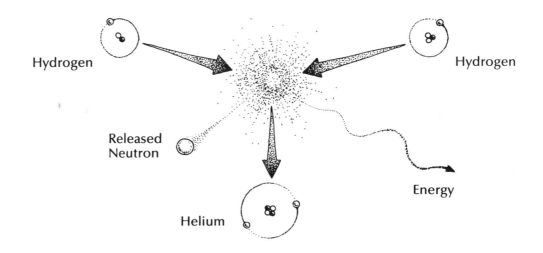

Hydrogen

Hydrogen

Released
Neutron

Energy

Helium

Our sun seems so much brighter and larger than other stars simply because it is much nearer to us. But all stars are constantly producing immense amounts of light and other forms of energy by fusing hydrogen atoms into helium.

Artificial Light
After the sun has set, we get most of our light from electric light bulbs, or lamps as they are more properly called. We also get light from fluorescent lamps, which are a special kind of electric light. They all provide what is called *artificial light*.

The history of artificial light goes back many thousands of years. Humans discovered that the flames of a fire produce light. In time they learned how to create light with the tiny fires in candles and oil lamps.

Candles and oil lamps work the same way. Both have a wick, a length of cord set in the wax or oil. When the wick is lit, the flame heats either the solid candle wax or the liquid oil. The heat changes the wax or oil into a gas. This hot gas then burns, producing light.

Candles are still in use today, but oil lamps have almost completely disappeared. Would you like to make a simple oil lamp? You'll need some cotton string, a metal cup or small pan, and any kind of liquid vegetable oil used for cooking or for making salads.

Cut off three 8-inch lengths of string. Braid them to make the wick. Place the wick in the cup or pan so that one end sticks up but does not hang over the edge. Pour in enough oil to cover most of the wick. Now place your oil lamp on a metal or stone surface for safety's sake. With the help of a grown-up, light the top end of the wick with a match. Watch the flame of your lamp cast a soft glow in the room— the same sort of light your ancestors saw very long ago.

Oil Lamp Experiment

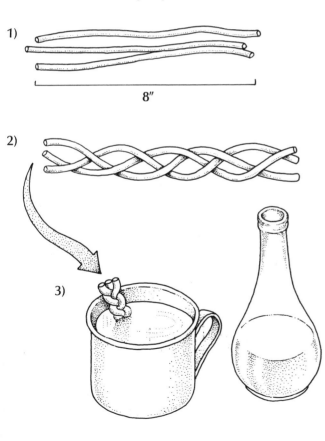

1)

8"

2)

3)

4)

Since the 1880s, the electric light lamp has replaced both the candle and the oil lamp as the main source of artificial light. The electric light lamp changes electrical energy into light energy. It is very easy to operate. You flip a switch and the light comes on. But how does this happen?

Flipping the switch sends a current of electricity through wires to the lamp. Inside the lamp the electricity flows through a length of very thin tungsten wire, called a *filament*. But the filament is too thin to carry the electricity so it overheats. In a flash it glows white hot. And you see this shine of the white-hot filament as light. But electric light lamps are very wasteful. Only about 5 percent of the electrical energy supplied to the bulb becomes light. The other 95 percent is changed to heat. You know this if you have ever burned your finger on a lit lamp.

Light Bulb

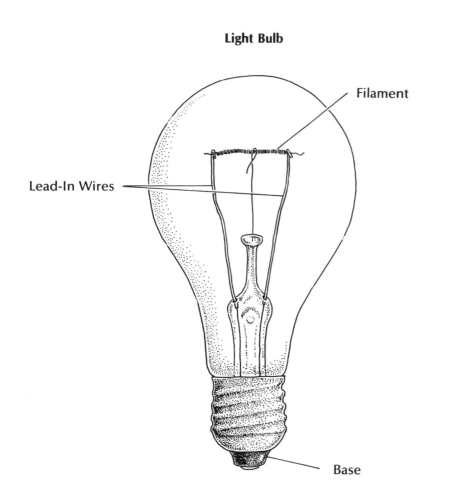

Filament

Lead-In Wires

Base

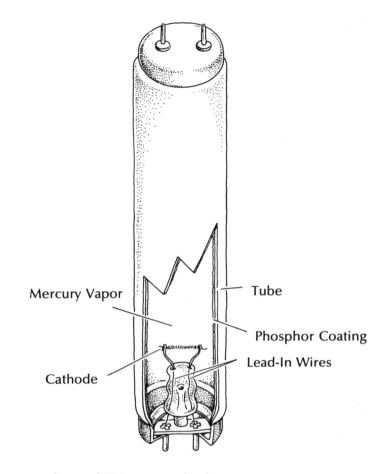

Mercury Vapor

Cathode

Tube

Phosphor Coating

Lead-In Wires

Fluorescent lights are much more efficient. With the same amount of electricity, they produce more light and less heat than the usual electric light lamps. The fluorescent tube contains mercury vapor. As electricity passes through the tube it causes the mercury atoms to emit ultraviolet rays. These rays strike certain chemicals, called *phosphors,* that coat the inside of the tube. These phosphors then give off the visible light you see.

Theater spotlights and powerful searchlights are also electric lights. But they produce their light in still another way. Each spotlight or searchlight contains two thin carbon rods with a short gap between their ends. When an electric current is sent through the rods, the electricity jumps across the gap as a bright, flaming spark, called an *arc.* These so-called arc lights are very powerful sources of illumination.

The numbers and controls on some stereo, radio and TV sets, and other electronic equipment are often outlined in a soft red or green light. This light comes from a source called LED, short for Light-Emitting Diode. The LED light comes from two attached layers of crystal material. One material normally has too many electrons; the other has too few. When the current flows, the extra electrons move to the side with fewer electrons, and this produces the familiar red light.

Many digital watches and calculators show their numbers as black lines against a gray background. The light source here is LCD, short for Liquid Crystal Display. A crystal is any material whose molecules are arranged in rigid, geometric patterns. Most crystals are solids. Some of the more familiar ones are grains of sugar and salt, jewels like diamonds and rubies, and snowflakes. There are, however, some liquid crystals. (Many of these liquid crystals have jaw-breaking names like p-Methoxybenzylidene-p'-butyl-aniline or 4-Cyano-4'-n-pentyl-biphenyl!) The molecules of the liquid crystals have the same sort of molecular arrangements as the solids, yet they can be poured like water.

In LCD, a thin layer of a liquid crystal is sandwiched between two sheets of glass. The glass is coated with a transparent film of metal. A pattern of seven short lines that form the number 8 are etched in the top glass. When a tiny electrical charge is applied to the short lines, it causes the liquid crystal to turn black and outline the numbers that show the exact time or the computation.

Biological Light

Perhaps the most mysterious light source of all is that given off by certain plants and animals. You have probably seen flashing lights of fireflies on summer evenings. The light they give off comes from within their own bodies. Called biological light, or *bioluminescence*, it is light produced without heat.

One of the most spectacular displays of bioluminescence occurs every September along certain Pacific coast beaches in California. Huge masses of bacteria wash up on shore, turning the surf a dark red. At night the bacteria cast a pale, green light on the water. A step in the wet sand leaves a shiny footprint. A kick sends out a shower of bright sparks.

In New Zealand there is a deep, dark cave whose roof is covered with thousands of tiny spots of light. Each light is from a tiny glowworm hanging down from the ceiling. The light attracts the insects on which the glowworm feeds.

Most bioluminescent animals and plants give off light of only one color. But the so-called railroad worm of South America glows in two colors. This striking creature has eleven glowing green spots along the length of its body. On its head it has a single white light. When it crawls along the ground on a dark night, it looks like a miniature train with headlight and lit windows!

Scientists are studying bioluminescence to learn more about this light that seems to require no heat. They now believe that bioluminescence is the result of chemical processes that go on in the tissues of certain animals and plants.

Reflected Light

Some objects are visible because they give off their own light. The sun, candles and oil lamps, electric light lamps, and even fireflies, are such light sources.

But most objects—pens and pencils, trees and flowers, for example—do not produce any light. They are visible only when an outside source of light is present. The light then strikes the object and is *reflected,* or thrown back. You see the object when its reflected light reaches your eyes.

A mirror is an excellent reflector of light. Most are flat pieces of glass covered on one side with a thin layer of silver or other shiny metal. The light hits the glass and passes through to the metal backing. This shiny surface reflects back nearly all of the light. This lets you see your image very clearly.

Reflected light is like a bouncing ball. If you drop a ball straight down, it bounces straight up. But if you throw the ball at an angle, it bounces up at an angle. The angle of the bounce is always equal to the angle of the throw.

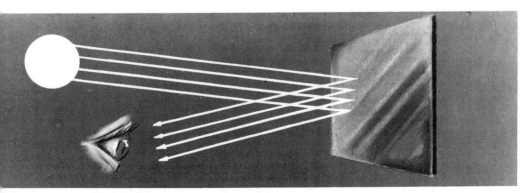

Light that strikes a mirror at an angle is reflected back at that same angle.

In the same way, light rays that strike a mirror straight on are reflected straight back. Those that strike at an angle are reflected back at that same angle. This is known as the *angle of reflection*.

To find a light ray's angle of reflection, collect a sheet of clear white paper, a small mirror, a thumbtack, a ruler, a protractor, and a pencil. Place the paper on a table, and then push the point of the thumbtack up through the paper about one or two inches in from the upper right corner. (The point of the thumbtack should be facing upward.) Move the paper so that the bottom edge is along the edge of the table.

Hold the mirror upright along the top edge of the paper. Position your head so that it is level with the table and to the left of the tack. Close one eye

Angle of Reflection Experiment

1)

2)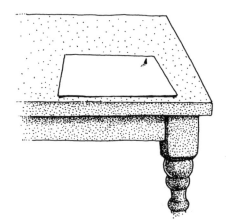

3)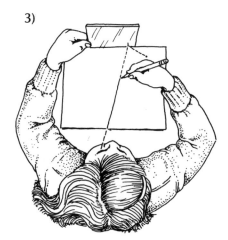

4)   Angle of Incidence = Angle of Reflection

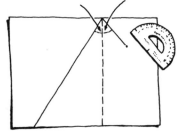

and draw a line from your open eye to the reflection of the tack in the mirror. Continue the line from that point to the actual tack. It should look like an upside down letter V, with one leg longer than the other.

Where the two lines of the V meet, use the ruler to draw a line perpendicular (at a right angle) to the top edge of the paper. With the protractor measure the angle between the line connecting the tack and reflection and the perpendicular line. That is called the *angle of reflection*. Then measure the angle between the line connecting your eye to the reflection and the perpendicular line. That is called the *angle of incidence*. You should find that the angle of reflection equals the angle of incidence.

Now look in a mirror and touch your right ear. It looks as though you're touching your *left* ear. Would you like to see yourself exactly as you look to others?

Get two small, purse-sized mirrors without frames. Hold them at right angles (90 degrees) to each other. Position yourself so that the reflection of your nose falls on the line between the two mirrors. Now touch your right ear again, and see yourself as everyone else sees you. The image of your right ear now appears in the mirror on your left, which is the right side of anyone facing you.

You know that you see this book because of reflected light. But what makes the words visible?

The words can be seen because different colors and surfaces reflect varying degrees of light. The white paper on which this book is printed, for example, reflects about 85 percent of the light that falls on it. The black ink with which the words are printed, though, reflects only about 3 percent of the light. Your eyes can easily sense the difference, making it possible to read the words.

What happens to the light that is not reflected by a dark surface? The light is taken in, or *absorbed*, by the surface.

You can prove this for yourself. Collect two small, clean, empty plastic margarine or cottage cheese tubs with lids. Paint them all over—one white,

Absorption Experiment

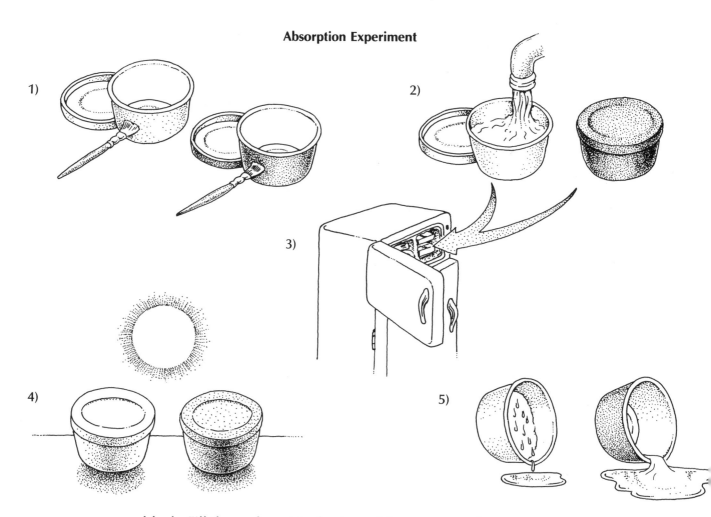

1)
2)
3)
4)
5)

one black. Fill them almost to the top with water, put the covers on, and set them in the refrigerator freezer overnight to turn the water into ice.

The next day set the two blocks of ice, still in the covered tubs, out in the sunlight. You'll notice that the ice in the black tub melts much faster than the ice in the white tub. The black color *absorbs* more of the sun's light energy and therefore gets warm faster. The white tub *reflects back* the sunlight, so it is not absorbed.

Materials differ in the amount of light that they reflect and absorb. Those with dark surfaces absorb much light and reflect only a little. Materials with light surfaces are just the opposite. They reflect most of the light without absorbing very much. Now you know why it is lighter outdoors on a night when there is snow on the ground. You can also understand why dark-colored clothes are hard to see at night.

Shadows

All of us view most objects either through the air or other materials that let light pass through easily. Air, glass and clear plastic all transmit light with little or no interference. They are said to be *transparent*. You can see clearly through transparent materials.

Frosted glass, clouds, thin sheets of paper, and some kinds of plastic are *translucent*. They allow some light to pass through but not enough to show clear details. The light does not pass through directly. It is scattered, or diffused, by the translucent material, making it hard to see details.

Most materials, though, are neither transparent nor translucent. They are *opaque*. No light can pass through an opaque object. Metal and wood, heavy cloth and paper, rocks and colored plastic are all opaque.

If an opaque object is in the path of a bright light, it casts a *shadow*. Hold an opaque object, such as your hand, in a beam of light. Your hand blocks some of the rays of light. A dark area, or shadow, forms in the shape of your hand. The other light rays go past your hand, creating a bright area around the shadow.

The closer the opaque object is to the source of light, the larger the shadow. As we said, light rays can be compared to the spokes radiating out from the hub of a bicycle wheel. The nearer to the hub you place your fist, the more spokes you cover. Covering more spokes is like blocking more beams of light. It makes the shadow appear bigger. The opposite is also true. The farther the object is from the source of light, the smaller the shadow.

The shadow of an object can be long or short. In a dimly lit room, stand an

The player casts a long shadow at after-school practice.

opaque object (a soda can works very well) upright on a flat, light-colored surface. Shine a flashlight from directly above the object. You'll see almost no shadow. Now, still aiming the beam at the object, slowly move the flashlight lower and lower along one side. Notice how the shadow grows longer and longer. When the flashlight is at the same level as the object, the shadow is as long as it can be.

To understand this think of a straight line from the source of light past the top of the object to the surface on which the object is standing. If the source of light is up nearly over the object, the line ends on the surface close to the base of the object. Since the shadow goes from the base of the object to where the line reaches the surface, the shadow is short. If the light source moves down lower and more to the side, though, the line—and light—strike the surface farther away. The shadow is longer. And the lower the light moves, the longer the shadow grows.

You can see long and short shadows on a sunny day. Shadows are long in the morning because the sun is low on the eastern horizon. They disappear almost completely by noon when the sun is close to directly overhead. And they become long again in the late afternoon as the sun sets on the western horizon.

How Light Travels

Around 1800 the English scientist Thomas Young (1773–1829) offered proof that light moves out, or *radiates,* in all directions from its source. This motion has been compared to that of waves spreading out when you drop a stone into a still body of water.

In 1864 another Englishman, James Clerk Maxwell (1831–1876), proposed a simple set of laws that showed the close relationship between electricity, magnetism and light. This so-called electromagnetic theory of light stated that visible light is only one of many types of electromagnetic radiation. There are electromagnetic rays of very long wavelength, such as cosmic rays, X rays and ultraviolet rays. And there are also electromagnetic rays of much shorter wavelength, including infrared (or heat) rays, and radio and television waves. Visible light is about halfway between the longest and shortest rays in wavelength.

At the beginning of this century, the German physicist Max Planck (1858–1947) added something more to the understanding of light. In his quantum theory Planck stated that light is given off in little bundles of energy instead of a steady stream. He called each bundle of energy a *quantum* (the plural is quanta).

According to Planck's theory, the amount of energy in each quantum depends on the length of the light waves. Each quantum, though, is so small and there are so many of them that there seems to be a steady flow. It is like water that moves in a stream even though it is made up of many separate drops.

Albert Einstein (1879–1955) gave the units, or quanta, of electromagnetic energy a new name. He called them *photons.*

Light travels at the tremendous speed of 186,000 miles per second. In fact, according to Einstein, nothing can travel faster than the speed of light. If someone turns on a light 100 feet from where you are standing, the light reaches your eyes in about one ten-millionth of a second! It takes the light of the sun, which is 93 million miles away, about eight minutes to arrive at the earth.

Light travels much faster than sound. When a batter hits a baseball in a large stadium, for example, you see it almost immediately. But you don't hear the crack of the bat for a fraction of a second because light zips along at 186,000 miles per second, while sound travels only about one-fifth of a mile per second.

You can also notice the difference in speed between light and sound during thunderstorms. Although the crash of thunder occurs at the same time as the bolt of lightning, you see the lightning before you hear the thunder. This time difference can tell you how far you are from the lightning.

During the next thunderstorm, try this little experiment. As soon as you see a flash of lightning, start counting seconds (one, one-thousand, two, one-thousand, three, one-thousand, etc.). Stop when you hear the thunder. Every 5 seconds equals about a mile of distance. Thus a count of 10 tells you that the center of the storm is approximately two miles away.

Astronomers use light as a ruler for measuring the immense distances in space. A *light-year* is the distance that light, moving at 186,000 miles per second, travels in one year. It is equal to about 6 trillion miles. Alpha Centauri, the star closest to the sun, is 4⅓ light-years from the sun. That means it is nearly 26 trillion miles away. The light that reaches your eyes today from the North Star has been traveling for several hundred years. The farthest stars are about 16 billion light-years away!

Measuring Light

We measure length by inches, temperature by degrees, time by minutes. But how do we measure light?

The early unit of light intensity, or brightness, was the *candle*. It was the light cast by a candle one inch in diameter. Over the years, though, the flickering candle flame was found to be too uncertain a standard for light measurement. In 1931 the new standard unit of light intensity became the *candela*. It is based on the bright, yellow-white light given off by the metal platinum when it is heated until it glows.

The unit of light output, or flux, is the *lumen*. A light that emits one candela in all directions emits about 12½ lumens. Electric light lamps should really be rated in lumens instead of watts. Watts indicate the power consumed, but not the light output. The usual 50-watt frosted lamp you use at home has an output of about 660 lumens; a 75-watt bulb produces 1,100 lumens, and a 100-watt bulb, 1,650 lumens.

A very important measurement unit is the amount of light, or *illumination*, on a surface, such as a book, table or road. The unit is the *footcandle*, which is the number of lumens per square foot. It is the illumination cast by a source of one candela intensity at a distance of one foot. For eating at a table, about 10 footcandles of illumination is enough. To read this book comfortably, you need about 15 footcandles on the page. Night baseball games require about 30 footcandles on the playing field. On a clear, bright day the sunlight provides about 10,000 footcandles of illumination.

Color

Have you ever seen a rainbow in the sky? Or have you ever seen the rainbow colors in diamonds and certain kinds of glass? in soap bubbles? in a water spray? in drops of automobile oil on the pavement?

Where do these colors come from?

Most of the light around us, such as sunlight, is white light. But white light is really a mixture of colors. It is made up of red, orange, yellow, green, blue, indigo, and violet. These colors make up the *spectrum*. All rainbows contain the spectrum of these seven colors in the same order.

You have probably seen a wedge of clear glass, called a *prism*. If you shine white light through the prism, the light that comes out has all the colors of the rainbow.

A rainbow is created whenever something splits the white light into its basic colors. The rainbow in the sky is created by tiny drops of water in the air breaking apart the sun's white light. The rainbow you see in a fine water spray is made in the same way. Diamonds and some pieces of glass reflect and bend the light in ways that separate it into the different colors. And colors show up in bubbles and oil films because the light is reflected from both the top and bottom surfaces of the bubble skin or oil film. The two, slightly different, reflected light waves bump into each other and create the colors.

You recall that light travels in waves. Each color has a different wavelength, which is measured by the distance from one crest to the next. The wavelengths of the different colors are all very short. Violet light has the shortest of all at only 1/60,000 of an inch. The lengths grow longer toward the red-light side of the spectrum, which has the longest, measuring about 1/30,000 of an inch from crest to crest.

Color depends on what you are looking at and what kind of light you see in it. White paper looks white because it reflects all the colors in sunlight. But if you shine a green light on the paper, it appears green. A house that is painted red looks red because the paint reflects the red in the sunlight and absorbs all the other colors.

Although sunlight is white, the sky appears blue. Why? The white sunlight is scattered by particles of dust and moisture in the earth's atmosphere. The particles scatter the shorter wavelengths more than the longer wavelengths. Since the shorter wavelengths are blue in color, the sky appears blue.

You can try this out. Fill a glass with water and add a few drops of milk. In a dark room shine a flashlight through a side of the glass. Look at the glass at a right angle to the flashlight beam. It will have a slightly blue color. The reason is that the particles of milk in the water scatter the shorter wave lengths of the flashlight beam just as the dust and moisture particles in the air scatter the shorter wavelengths of the sun's rays.

You can combine all the colors to produce white in this experiment. Cut out a four-inch disk of white cardboard. Paint a pie-shaped wedge of each of the seven colors of the spectrum on the disk.

Color Experiment

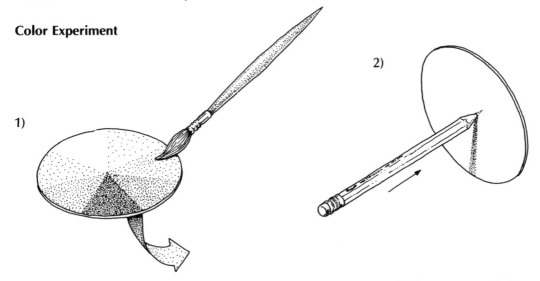

Now push the sharp point of a long pencil up through the center of the disk. Rub the pencil between your open palms and see the colors blend together into a whitish blur. Your eyes cannot see each individual color as they mix together to create white.

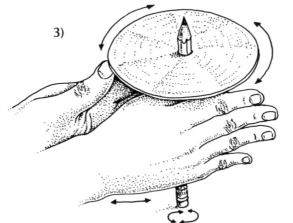

Cascade Junior High School
Library

Every color has three qualities. The particular color—red, green, blue, and so on—is called the *hue*. The *brightness* or *value* describes the darkness or lightness of the color. And the *chroma* or *saturation* places the color on a scale of intensity that goes from weak to vivid.

The American painter Albert H. Munsell (1858–1918) devised what he called a *color tree* to introduce a system for the use of color. The central trunk of the color tree is a thin column that shows the scale of brightness, ranging from black to white. Arranged radially around the trunk are the hues—red, orange, yellow, and so forth. Each branch shows the chroma going from very weak at the trunk to very strong at the end. Munsell assigned a number to each spot on the color tree. With the Munsell color tree, it is possible to express a color exactly by a number.

2.
Lenses

Lenses are curved pieces of transparent material, such as glass or clear plastic, that bend the rays of light passing through them.

Lenses have many important uses in modern life. The lens in your eye lets you see the world around you. Eyeglasses, contact lenses and magnifying glasses help you to see better. The lenses in microscopes and telescopes make it possible to see the very small and the very distant. Slide and movie projector lenses make it possible for many people to see the same pictures at the same time. And camera lenses allow you to take clear, distinct photographs of objects near and far.

Pencil in Water Experiment

How Do Lenses Work?
All lenses work the same way. They all bend, or *refract*, beams of light. Light is refracted because it travels through different transparent materials at various speeds. As a light beam passes from one material to another, it actually changes direction.

You can see the refraction of light waves in this experiment. Put a long pencil into half a glass of water. Look at the pencil from the side. Does it look like the pencil is broken at the water line?

Light travels through air at 186,000 miles per second but through water at 140,000 miles per second. When you look at the pencil, you see the top part through the air. But you see the lower part through the air *and* through the water. Because the light bends as it goes from one medium to another, the pencil looks like it has two distinct parts.

You can use the principle of light refraction to fool a friend. First ask whether he or she thinks a penny can float. The answer will probably be no. Then drop a penny into a small bowl. Tell your friend to raise the bowl until the penny just disappears from his or her sight. Now slowly pour water into the bowl. Soon your friend will see the penny "float" into view.

Of course, the penny does not actually float. But the light, passing from water to air, is bent so that it makes the penny appear to be floating on the water.

The Shape of Lenses

Lenses come in two basic shapes—*concave* and *convex*. Lenses that are thin in the middle and thick at the edges are concave. Lenses that are thick in the middle and thin at the edges are convex. (An easy way to remember the difference is that concave lenses look "caved" in at the center.)

The concave lens is thin in the center and spreads rays of light.

A convex lens is thick in the center and brings rays of light together.

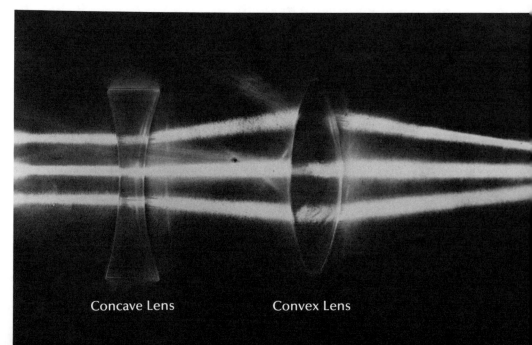

Concave Lens   Convex Lens

Because of the difference in shape, the two types of lenses have opposite effects on light. A concave lens spreads out the rays of light that pass through. A convex lens brings together rays of light.

Since a concave lens is thinner in the middle than around the edge, it causes the beams of light to spread out, or *diverge*. Diverging rays of light make objects appear smaller than they really are.

This experiment will show you how a concave lens makes the light rays diverge. You'll need a comb, a flashlight and a concave lens. If you don't have a concave lens, ask to borrow the eyeglasses of someone who is nearsighted.

In a dark room, hold the comb, teeth up, on a table. First shine the flashlight beam through the teeth of the comb and notice the shadows of the teeth on the table. Next place the lens between the flashlight and the comb. Now you'll see that the shadows of the teeth are spread farther apart. This shows that the concave lens causes light beams to diverge.

Concave Lens Experiment

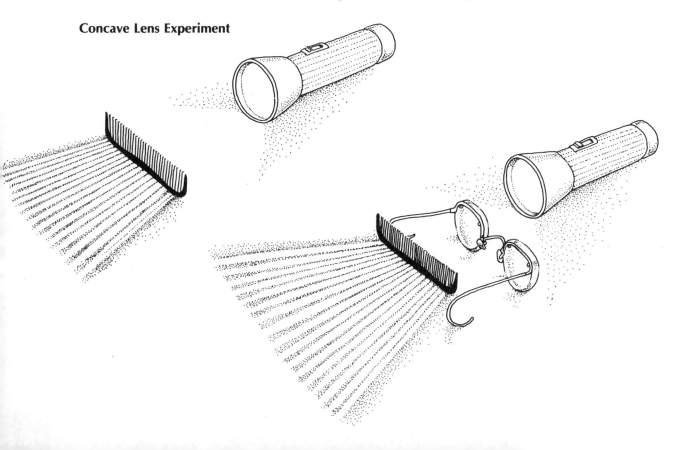

Concave lenses come in three shapes. Lenses that are pinched in on both front and back are *double concave*. Such lenses are used when a small, reduced image is wanted. Those that are pinched in on one side but flat on the other, are called *plano-concave*. Cameras make use of plano-concave lenses. And if the lens is curved on both sides, but still thinner in the middle than at the edges, it is called *concavo-convex*. Eyeglasses for people who are nearsighted have these lenses.

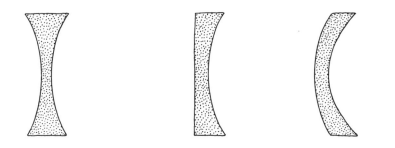

1) Double Concave   2) Plano-Concave   3) Concavo-Convex

When light beams enter a convex lens, they are refracted on entering and refracted again on leaving. Those passing through near the edges of the lenses are bent sharply; those near the center are bent slightly. As a result, all the light rays come together, or *converge*. The point at which the rays converge is called the *focus*. The distance from the lens to the focus is the *focal length*.

Humans learned very long ago that objects seen through convex lenses appear larger than they really are. Probably the earliest convex lens was nothing more than a drop of water. Later lenses were small, round balls of glass. Most lenses today are disks shaped out of glass or clear plastic.

You can see how a drop of water works as a convex lens to magnify an image. Cut out a 3-inch square of plastic wrap. Holding it along two sides, drip a tiny bit of water into the center so that it forms a single round drop of water. Lower the plastic over a printed word in a newspaper or magazine. Notice how the letters look larger through the water-lens than through the air.

Knowing this, can you guess why certain food products are packed in round jars? Olives, for example, are almost always sold in round jars filled with water. The water in the round jar acts as a convex lens. It makes the olives look larger than they really are. If you look through the flat bottom of the jar, you'll notice that the olives look the "right" size.

A lens that is thicker in the middle on both sides is properly called *double convex*. Most magnifying glasses are double convex lenses. If a lens bulges on only one side, and is flat on the other side, it is known as *plano-convex*. Plano-convex lenses are used in slide and movie projectors. Lenses that are shaped like a new moon or like the letter "C," but are thick in the middle, are *convexo-concave*. You find them in eyeglasses worn by people who are farsighted. All the different types of convex lenses refract the light to make objects appear larger and clearer.

1) Double Convex   2) Plano-Convex   3) Convexo-Concave

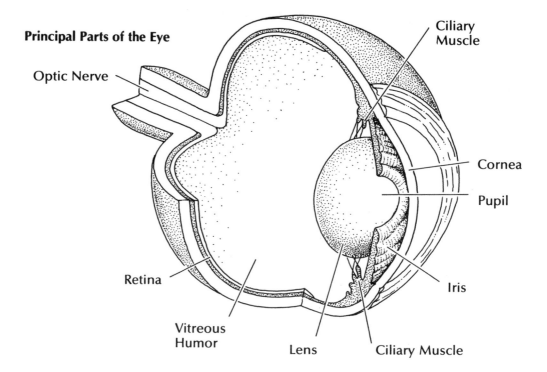

Principal Parts of the Eye

Optic Nerve

Ciliary Muscle

Cornea

Pupil

Retina

Iris

Vitreous Humor

Lens

Ciliary Muscle

The Lens in Your Eye

The human organ of sight is, of course, the eye. Your eye is shaped like a ball. It is filled with a transparent jelly-like substance known as *vitreous humor*. Covering the front part of the eye is the transparent *cornea*. Directly behind the cornea is a colored disk, called the *iris*, with a dark, round opening, called the *pupil*. Muscles open and close the iris to change the size of the pupil. This controls the amount of light that can enter the eye.

Just behind the pupil is a *double convex lens* through which light enters your eye. Made of clear tissue, the lens acts like a magnifying glass. It brings to a focus the rays of light that pass through the cornea and the pupil. If the lens is properly shaped, it forms a sharp image on the inner lining of the eyeball, called the *retina*. When rays of light strike the light-sensitive cells of the retina, they send tiny electrical impulses along the *optic nerve* to the brain. The images formed on the retina are always upside down. But the brain interprets the images so that we see everything right side up.

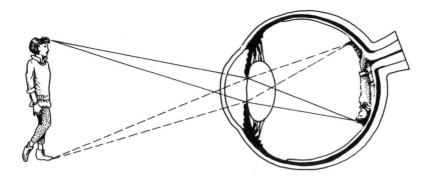

The image that forms on the retina is upside down.

The lens in your eye has a difficult job to perform. The lens has to bring the words in this book to a focus, at a distance of about 18 inches from your eye. But the same lens has to be able to focus on road signs that might be as far away as 1800 feet or more. How does the lens manage to focus on both near and far objects, as well as on everything in between?

To see objects at different distances, the lens in your eyes actually changes its shape. This ability to change is called *accommodation*. Tiny muscles in the eye, called *ciliary muscles,* can pull on the lens in one way or another to make the lens thicker or thinner. To see things that are close by, the muscles make the lens thicker. For more distant objects, the lens is made thinner, or flatter.

Here's how you can feel the ciliary muscles changing the shape of your lens. Shut one eye and hold a pencil in front of the other eye at a distance of about 8 inches. Focus on the pencil. Then focus on some distant object directly behind the pencil. Do you feel a change inside your eye as you change the focus? Do you also notice that when your eyes focus on a nearby object things that are far away are out of focus? And vice versa?

There is a limit, though, to how much the human lens can accommodate. That is why it is sometimes hard to read words that are too close or too far away.

You can test your own accommodation limits. Place this book open on the floor. Raise your head above the book until you can no longer make out the words. (You may have to stand on a chair.) Use a tape measure or yardstick to measure the distance. Now slowly lower your head toward the book. Stop when you are so close that you can't read the words. What is the distance from your eyes to the page? The figures for distant and close measurement give you the approximate limits of accommodation of your lens.

Some people, though, cannot see things sharply. There are those who can see things close up perfectly, but cannot form clear images of distant objects. They are said to be *nearsighted*. Nearsightedness may be caused by an eyeball that is too long from front to back. Or it may be caused by a lens that is too convex. In either case, rays of light from distant objects come to a focus in front of the retina.

Nearsighted people can correct their problem by wearing glasses with slightly concave lenses. These lenses bend rays of light so that they come to a focus farther back and onto the retina. The nearsighted are then able to see sharp images of distant objects.

Those who are *farsighted* can see faraway objects well, but cannot form sharp images of things close up. The condition may be caused by an eyeball that is too short or by a lens that is not convex enough. In either case, rays of light from close objects come to a focus behind the retina. Many older people become farsighted since the lenses usually become less flexible with age and cannot become as thick as they could before. To correct farsightedness, a person can wear glasses with slightly convex lenses. These bend the rays of light so that they come to a focus directly on the retina.

Some people cannot see clearly unless the object is very close.

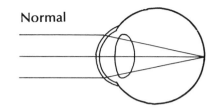

Normal

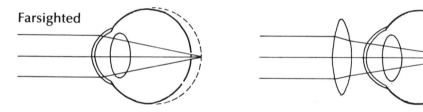

Nearsighted

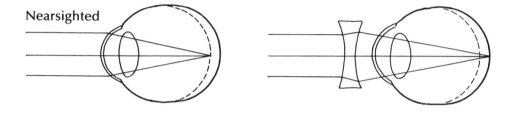

Farsighted

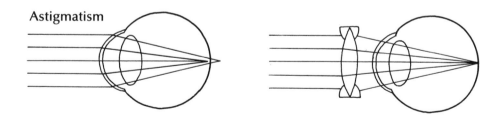

Astigmatism

Different lenses can help those who are nearsighted, farsighted or astigmatic.

Astigmatism causes things to look strange.

Astigmatism is a condition in which a person sees clearly in some parts of his field of vision but with blurring in other parts. Astigmatism is usually caused by an uneven curve of the lens. Eyeglasses with special lenses can make the entire field of vision clear and distinct.

Contact lenses are a type of eyeglass placed directly on the eyeball to correct defects in vision. Although they were first made of glass and then hard plastic, many are now made of soft, thin plastic that can be worn for several weeks before needing a cleaning.

When people have trouble seeing and think they may need glasses, they go to an "eye doctor." There are actually three types of professionals in-

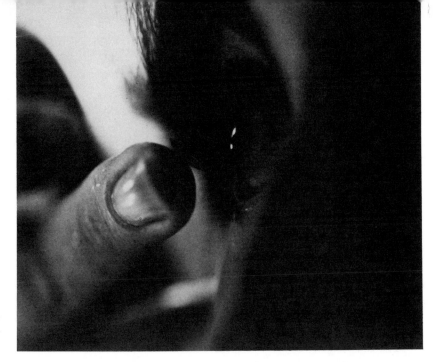

The contact lens is placed directly on the eyeball.

volved in eye care. *Ophthalmologists* are highly trained medical doctors who specialize in the eye. Besides determining whether a person needs glasses, ophthalmologists also treat diseases and injuries of the eyes. Although they are not medical doctors, *optometrists* are doctors trained to test eyes and prescribe corrective lenses. And *opticians* are the ones who prepare the glasses. They prepare the lenses according to the prescription of the ophthalmologist or optometrist and make sure that the glasses fit the patient.

The Camera Lens

Basically, a camera works much like an eye. The camera lens gathers light and focuses an image upside down on the film against the back wall of the camera. Your eye changes its focus by changing the focal length of its lens. You change the focus of the camera by turning the focusing knob, which moves the lens toward or away from the film. Some advanced cameras adjust the focal length automatically. Other, more basic cameras have no focusing adjustment. They are permanently focused on objects that are at least 10 feet away.

Your eye adjusts to varying light conditions by changing the size of the pupil opening. On most cameras there is a *diaphragm* near the lens that opens and closes, allowing more or less light to enter the camera.

While your eyes stay open most of the time, the camera *shutter* opens very briefly when you snap a picture. By flicking open for only a fraction of a second, the camera is able to freeze the motion of even fast-moving people or objects.

Magnifying Glass

You have probably used a magnifying glass at home or in school. As you know, magnifying glasses are double convex lenses that make objects appear larger. People use magnifying glasses to see tiny details that are not clearly visible to the naked eye.

Magnifying glasses differ in their *magnifying power,* or *magnification,* according to the exact shape of the lens. The magnifying power is the number of times larger the image appears to be than the actual size of the object. Here is how you find out the magnifying power of a glass. Place the magnifying glass on a flat ruler so that the center of the glass is on the measuring

Some people need to use a magnifying glass to read a newspaper.

edge of the ruler. Count the number of eighth-inch markers you can see. Write down the number.

Next, without moving your eye, raise the glass until you get the largest, most distinct image. Count the number of eighth-inch markers you can now see through the glass. Write down this number and then divide the original number by this magnified number. The resulting figure is the magnifying power. Try this with different magnifying glasses. The higher the magnifying power, the greater the magnification.

People usually look through magnifying glasses to see something better. But you can also use a magnifying glass to project an image. Stand with your back to a window. With one hand hold up a blank sheet of white paper; with the other, hold a magnifying glass between the paper and the window. Move the glass back and forth until you get a clear image on the paper. The image should be sharp and distinct, but you'll notice that it is upside down.

With the help of a friend, measure the distance from the magnifying glass to the paper. This is the focal length of the glass. Here is how you can use this figure to show how a simple magnifying glass can be used to provide a variety of images.

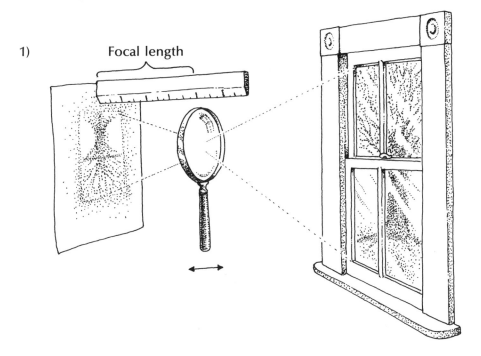

1) Focal length

In a darkened room, open a newspaper on a table. Use some clay to hold your magnifying glass erect in the middle of the paper. Draw a straight line that extends both in front and behind the glass. On both segments of the line measure out and mark both the focal length (F) and double the focal length (2F).

Place yourself by one end of the line looking toward the glass, and put a candle about 2 inches beyond 2F in front of the glass. Hold a piece of typing paper behind the glass and between F and 2F on that side. Move it back and forth until you get a sharp image.

You'll see that the image of the candle is smaller than the original candle and that it is inverted, or upside down. The lens systems in cameras work in this way. If you think of replacing the paper with film, you can see how the film captures the image.

Next move the candle to the 2F position, but keep the paper in the same place. The image is still inverted, but this time it is the same size as the original candle. Some telescopes include a lens that is used in this way.

What happens when you place the candle between F and 2F? The image is clearest when the paper is behind the 2F mark. It is still inverted, but it is larger than the original. The lens systems of slide and movie projectors cast a large image on a screen this way. Other lenses in the projector turn the image rightside up.

If you place the candle exactly at the focal point, you will not be able to get any image on the paper. An object at the focal point of a lens does not form an image since the rays are all parallel and therefore do not come to a point.

Finally, position the candle between the glass and F. Again you'll see no image on the paper. But if you look through the looking glass in the other direction, at the candle, you will see an image. It is larger than the original, not inverted and appears between F and 2F in front of the glass. This is actually what you see when you use a magnifying glass in the usual way.

2)

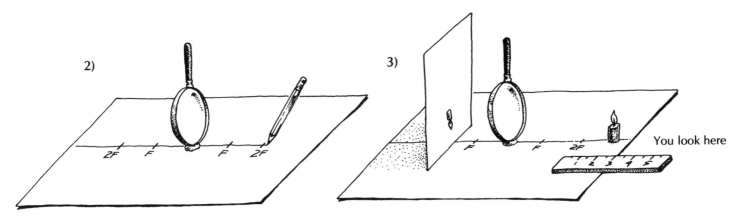

2F F F 2F

3)

F F 2F

You look here

1 2 3 4 5

4)

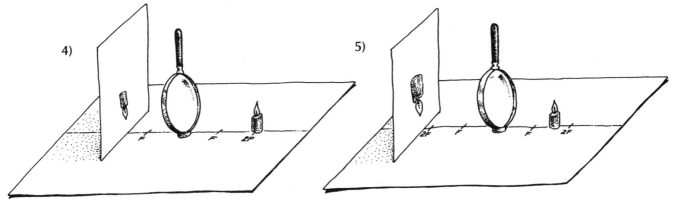

F F 2F

5)

2F F F 2F

6)

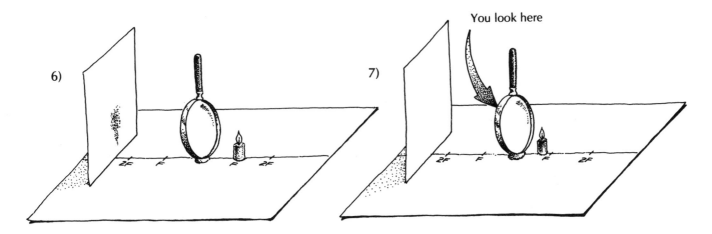

2F F F 2F

7)

You look here

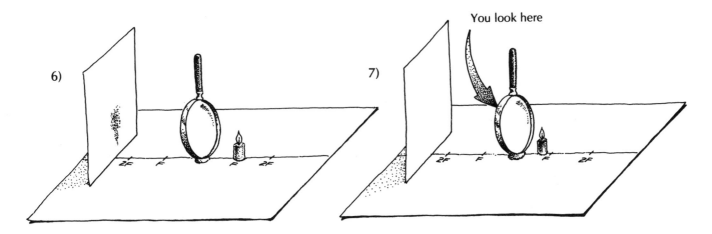

2F F F 2F

Microscopes and Telescopes

The microscope is a scientific instrument that uses lenses to magnify objects. It makes it possible to see details that are normally invisible to the naked eye. A magnifying glass is a simple microscope. But magnifying glasses seldom have a magnification greater than 10. For greater magnification you need a compound microscope, with two or more separate lenses.

In a compound microscope, there are two convex lenses or groups of lenses. They are placed at opposite ends of a tube. One lens is located at the bottom of the tube just above the object being viewed. Called the *objective lens,* it creates a larger image of the object. The upper lens is the *eyepiece lens.* The eyepiece lens magnifies the image from the objective lens as much as 2,000 times.

While the microscope is used to examine the very small, the telescope helps us to see the very distant. Like the microscope, the telescope uses two lenses. But instead of both being convex, the one at the far end of the tube (the objective lens) is convex, and the one near the eye (the eyepiece lens) is concave.

According to a frequently told story, the idea of combining the two lenses occurred by accident. In 1608 the Dutch optician, Hans Lippershey (c. 1570–1619) was testing some lenses in the light of a window. He happened to hold a convex lens far from his eyes and a concave one near his eyes at the same time. As he looked through the two lenses he noticed that distant objects—a church steeple, a windmill—appeared much larger and closer than ever before.

The following year, Galileo (1564–1642), the Italian astronomer, built the first telescope. The crude instrument had two lenses attached at the opposite ends of a long cardboard tube. His most powerful telescope magnified objects only thirty-three times. Nevertheless, with it he could see the rings of Saturn, the satellites of Jupiter, and the mountains on the moon.

The simple telescope used by Galileo and other astronomers is called the *refracting telescope.* A large convex lens at the far end of the tube gathers

Compound Microscope

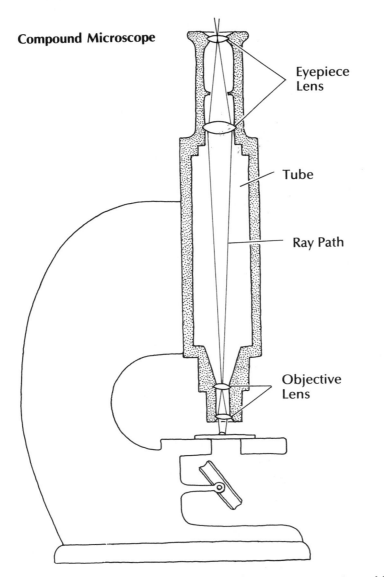

Eyepiece
Lens

Tube

Ray Path

Objective
Lens

light from a star, for example. The lens bends the light rays and brings them to a focus at the eyepiece. The concave eyepiece lens then magnifies the image and makes it appear very close. But the image appears upside down. Where it is necessary to see the image rightside up, a special lens is placed between the two lenses to invert the image.

The largest refracting telescope is at the Yerkes Observatory at Williams Bay, Wisconsin. The tube is 62 feet long and the lenses each have a diameter of 40 inches.

The largest refracting telescope is at the Yerkes Observatory in Williams Bay, Wisconsin.

The largest reflecting telescope is the Hale telescope on Mount Palomar, California. Notice the 200-inch mirror at the end of the tube and the man seated at the focus point.

The second type of telescope that astronomers use is the *reflecting telescope*. Instead of glass lenses, there is one large slightly curved mirror at the bottom of the tube. The mirror gathers light from the object and brings it to a focus on a small second mirror at the center of the telescope. This mirror reflects the image through the side of the tube to the eyepiece. The largest reflecting telescope is the Hale telescope on Mount Palomar in California. This telescope has a reflecting mirror 200 inches in diameter.

A third type of telescope, the *radio telescope*, does not use lenses or mirrors or light at all. It is nothing more than a huge antenna that picks up the natural radio signals that are being emitted by various celestial bodies and gases in space.

A radio telescope uses no lenses or mirrors. It is really just a huge antenna.

3.
Lasers

A laser is a device that produces a very special kind of light. Laser light is extremely *intense*. Some laser light is even brighter and more brilliant than sunlight. Laser light also shines in a *narrow beam* that does not spread out like ordinary light.

Imagine shining a flashlight outdoors on a dark night. The light spreads out so much that its beam doesn't reach beyond a few dozen feet. Then consider that in 1962 a laser beam was aimed at the moon, 250,000 miles away. It created a circle of light on the moon that was only 2½ miles wide, and that could be seen from earth!

Perhaps most important is that laser light waves are tightly organized, or *coherent*. They are different from ordinary light waves, which start at different times and go off every which way. Laser light waves all move together in only one direction.

Picture the exit gate of a big stadium at the end of a football game. The fans pour out and head off in all directions, some running and some walking. That is like ordinary light. Now imagine a marching band coming out from the same gate. They are in step and all moving together at the same speed. Their movement can be compared to laser light.

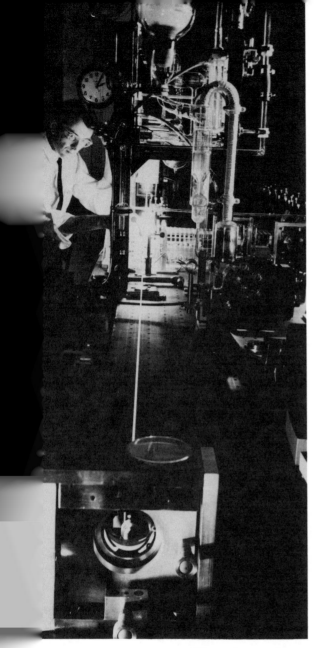

The laser beam shooting down the middle of this photograph is intense and narrow.

Dr. Theodore H. Maiman made the first laser in 1960.

Finally, laser light is of only one color, or *monochromatic*. Ordinary light looks white, but is really made up of all the colors of the spectrum. But the light from a laser contains light of only one wavelength.

What's In a Name?

Laser is a made-up word formed from the first letters of: Light Amplification by Stimulated Emission of Radiation. If we take a close look at each of these words we'll understand the special nature of lasers.

Light. As you know, all light is a form of electromagnetic radiation that is visible to the human eye.

Amplification. Amplification is simply the process of making something bigger or more powerful. When you turn up the volume on a radio, you are amplifying the sound. With lasers, amplification makes the light brighter.

Stimulated. To stimulate means to stir to action. Laser light is created when a burst of light or electricity excites the atoms in the laser to emit photons. These photons then stimulate the creation of additional identical photons to produce the bright laser light.

Emission. This refers to something that is sent out or given off. Stimulated laser emission consists of large numbers of photons that create the intense, narrow, coherent, monochromatic laser light.

Radiation. The laser light is a form of energy that radiates, or moves out, from the laser source.

The First Laser

Dr. Theodore H. Maiman (b. 1927), working at the Hughes Research Laboratories in Malibu, California, made the very first laser on May 15, 1960.

The heart of Dr. Maiman's laser was a crystal gem—a ruby. Instead of a natural gem, though, which has too many defects, Maiman used a synthetic (man-made) ruby. The ruby was a clear, pink-colored round rod less than one inch long and a half inch in diameter.

Cascade Junior High School
Library
Auburn, WA

21533

Around the rod Dr. Maiman twisted the hollow glass tubing of a flash lamp. A flash lamp gives short bursts of very intense light, much like the flash attachment on a camera. The pulse of light from the flash lamp excited the atoms within the ruby rod, causing them to emit a burst of photons.

Dr. Maiman had a very clever way of amplifying the photons within the ruby. He put a thin coating of silver on the ends of the ruby rod. Both ends reflected the photons so they would flash back and forth within the ruby at the speed of light. This stimulated other atoms to emit identical photons. On one end, though, he made a one millimeter (4/100ths of an inch) hole to allow some of the amplified light to escape. And it was this escaping light that became the world's first laser. Each short pulse of light from the ruby had an amazing 10,000 watts of power.

Since that day in 1960, lasers have undergone many changes and improvements. Ruby lasers are still being used. But now there are other crystal lasers, as well as those based on gases, semiconductors and liquids.

Kinds of Lasers

The original ruby laser is typical of all *crystal* or *glass lasers*. Such devices are usually excited with an intense light. The bright red light that they emit has enough energy to drill a small hole in a sheet of metal or even a diamond.

The more popular material used in crystal lasers today is known as YAG, short for yttrium-aluminum garnet. While ruby lasers can produce only short bursts of light, YAG emits a continuous beam. It is mainly used for drilling holes in metal and locating targets for military gunners.

Many lasers use a gas as the source of light. The most common *gas laser* works on a mixture of two gases, helium and neon. Called HeNe, the laser has metal electrodes at either end of the tube containing the gas. The atoms are excited by passing an electric current through the gas instead of exciting them with a light source.

The HeNe laser produces a red beam of light that is not very powerful. The lasers found in most school laboratories are HeNe lasers. They are also used

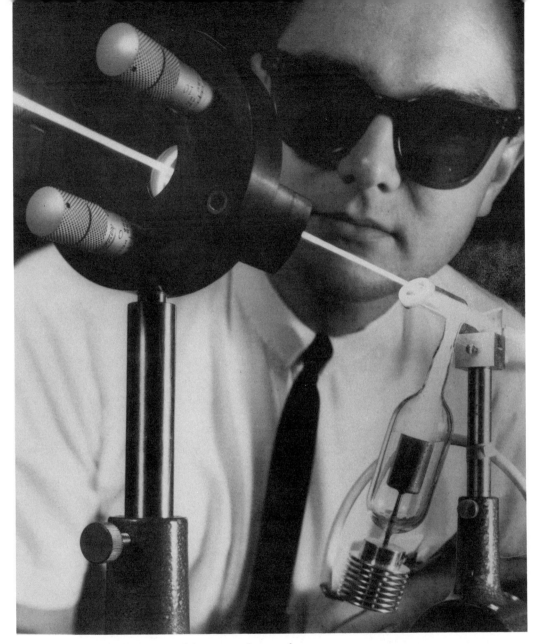

A scientist experiments with an early gas laser.

at supermarket and clothing store checkout counters and in libraries to read the code stripes on various products or books.

Another type of gas laser uses carbon dioxide (CO_2). Sometimes referred to as the "workhorse laser," it is commonly found in factories. Although the CO_2 laser can be very powerful, its beam is actually invisible. It is pure heat, or infrared, radiation. So great is its heat, though, that its main use is to weld together separate metal parts.

Do you recall the light source LED? It is the light that is produced when an electric current is applied to the two layers of a semiconductor. This same device is used to make a *semiconductor laser*. The light comes from the junction where the two materials meet. This is a very flat surface that acts like a mirror, reflecting the light back and forth, just like the mirrors at the ends of a crystal laser. When enough electricity is applied to the semiconductor, it emits a laser light.

Semiconductors are probably the most popular subject of today's laser research. Scientists see the great promise they hold. Semiconductor lasers are tiny; some are the size of a grain of salt. Researchers who work with

This photograph shows a tiny semiconductor laser amidst crystals of ordinary table salt.

A researcher uses a laboratory liquid laser.

them joke that if they're not careful they might inhale one! Present semiconductor lasers can emit light for a million hours, which is about 100 years. But experimenters are now talking of lasers that will last for millions of years. And semiconductor lasers are ideal for fiber optics, one of the exciting new laser applications that we will discuss.

The final group of lasers is the *liquid lasers*. In most of these the liquid is actually a dye. The dye offers the big advantage of being able to create a laser light of any color desired. Liquid lasers so far have found their greatest use in laboratories where specific colors are needed in order to analyze different chemical substances.

Back in 1977, Dr. John Madey of Stanford University built a completely different kind of laser. He called it the Free Electron Laser, or FEL. In the FEL, a beam of electrons is accelerated by passing through several powerful magnetic fields. The electron beam is then fired into a "wiggler," a device in which high-power electromagnets pull the electrons back and forth as they move forward. As each electron makes a sharp turn it emits a photon. The billions of electrons passing through send out enough photons to produce a superpowerful laser light. Because of its great power and efficiency, many scientists, like physicist and laser expert, Dr. John D. Rather, feel that in time the FEL "will change the world as much as the invention of electricity."

How Lasers are Used

In the 1960s the laser was called "a solution looking for a problem." Today, less than 30 years later, it is widely used in a broad range of fields. Among the more popular laser applications are those in communications, medicine, the military, industry, measuring, nuclear fusion, reading, compact discs and holography.

Communications

Laser beams can now carry telephone, radio or television signals through the air over great distances. What's more, many messages and programs can all be transmitted on a single laser beam at the same time. Its highly directional beam also makes it a particularly good transmitter for communications in space. In particular, researchers are now studying how laser beams can be used to link spacecraft with earth.

The most promising laser beam communication system, though, is one that transmits information through very thin glass fibers. The system is called *fiber optics.*

The information can be sent through the glass fiber in two different ways. The *analog* format produces a light signal that carries the information by varying the brightness of the light wave. This is the same as sending a sound

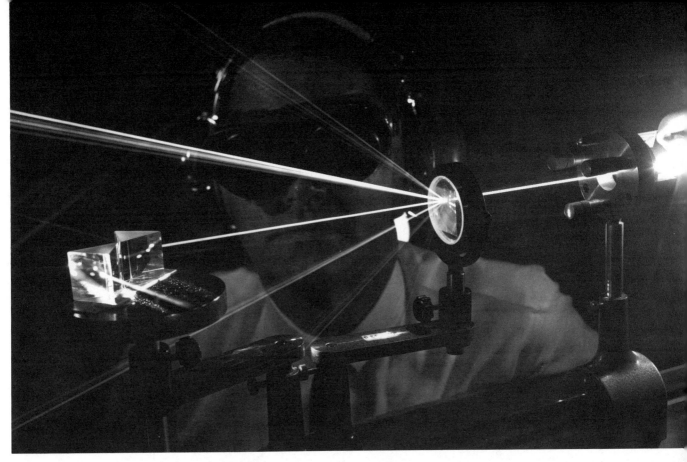

Laser beams can be used to send signals.

signal by varying the shape of the sound wave. The *digital* format translates the information into a pattern of very short, rapid on-and-off bursts of the laser light. The *ons* and *offs* of the digital format can be compared to the dots and dashes of the Morse code. The quick pulses of light are a code for the message that is being sent.

To understand how fiber optics work, imagine that you're making a telephone call. You speak into your home telephone. The equipment changes the vibrations of your voice into a varying electrical current that copies the pattern of the sound waves. This flow of electricity is used to excite a laser.

The laser in turn sends out either an analog or a digital light pattern that follows the pattern of the electrical flow.

The light speeds through the fiber at over 100,000 miles per second to the phone of the person at the other end of the line. Here the light pattern strikes a *photodetector,* which changes it back into electricity and then into sound.

The fibers are made of pure, flawless glass. They are unbelievably thin, around 5/1,000ths of an inch thick or one half the diameter of a human hair. Nevertheless, each fiber is twice as strong as steel and is able to withstand a pull of up to 600,000 pounds per square inch.

Two different kinds of glass actually make up the fiber. The inside, or *core,* is glass through which light easily passes. Surrounding it is the *cladding,* glass which reflects back any rays of light that escape from the core.

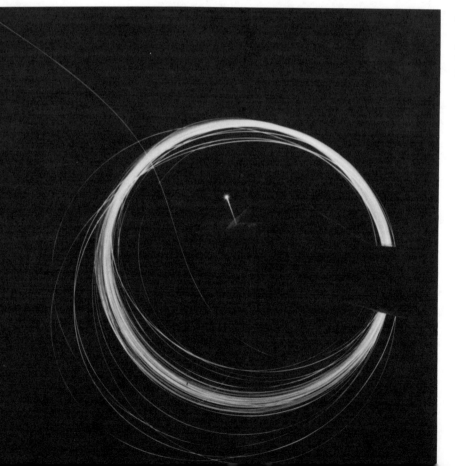

A new communication system sends laser light through very thin, long glass fibers.

Any laser source can be used to send light through the fiber. But most often the light comes from a semiconductor laser. The laser beam goes directly into the fiber and flashes down its length. Like all light, laser beams travel only in straight lines. One of the big advantages of the optical fiber is that it can bend and carry the laser beam around curves. When the beam comes to a turning in the fiber, it shoots out of the core and strikes the cladding. But the cladding reflects it right back into the core so that it can continue on its way.

Here's how you can bend a beam of ordinary light, using a stream of water instead of fiber optics. All you need is a clean, empty glass jar with a screw-on cap, a piece of dark cloth or dark paper (a supermarket bag will do), and a flashlight.

With a large nail, punch two holes in the cap, one at the center, the other near the rim. Fill the jar with water, and screw the cap on tightly. Now wrap the dark cloth or paper around the jar. Let most of the wrapping extend out like a sleeve from the bottom of the jar.

Bending Light Experiment

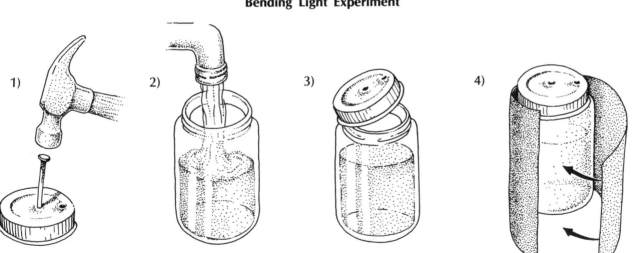

1) 2) 3) 4)

Hold the jar over a sink in a darkened room. Turn on the flashlight and shine it inside the dark sleeve against the bottom of the jar. Now tilt the jar so that the water flows out of the hole near the rim, with the center hole above it.

Do you see how the curved stream of water glows with light? Can you find the bright spot where the water hits the sink? Ask a friend to hold a hand in the stream. Does his or her hand glow in the light?

The stream of water is like the cladding in the fiber. It reflects back the straight light rays so that the light follows the curve of the stream.

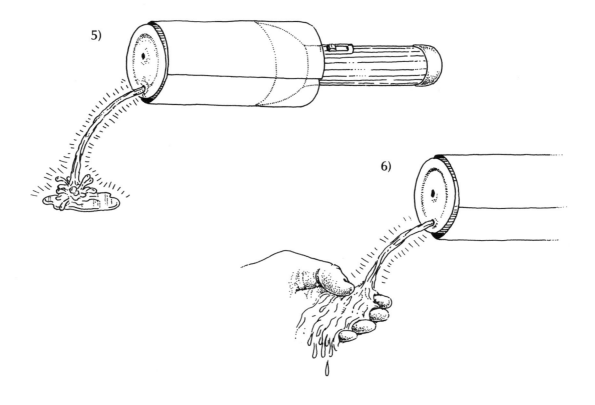

There are 144 glass fibers in a cable. They can carry 50,000 messages at the same time.

Glass fibers work better than the usual copper wires in communication systems. First they are cheaper and easier to handle. Second, 144 glass fibers in a single cable that is smaller than the diameter of a finger can carry over 50,000 messages at once—a task that would require over 4,000 copper wires in a cable 4½ inches wide! And finally, glass fibers transmit signals at very high speeds, with no danger of interference.

At its headquarters in Langley, Virginia, the Central Intelligence Agency (CIA) uses fiber optics to connect its telephones and computers. The reason is simple. If someone tries to tap into a fiber-optic communication line, the fiber itself is destroyed. In this way the CIA immediately knows if anyone is tampering with their information system.

Like other forms of energy, light signals grow weaker with distance. To travel very far they need to be boosted, or made stronger, with a *repeater*.

Copper wires require a booster every mile or so. Fiber-optic systems presently need repeaters every 4 miles. But new systems are now being developed that can space the repeaters about 12 miles apart.

Medicine

Surgeons use the heat of a sharp beam of laser light to perform certain types of operations. The light is most often from a CO_2 laser. The laser makes a clear cut without damaging the surrounding tissue. For some surgical procedures, like completely destroying cancerous growths, a more powerful YAG laser is used.

The surgeon focuses the beam to a very fine point. He or she then slowly moves the beam across the tissue. The laser vaporizes the tissue along that line, cleanly and sharply. At the same time, the heat of the laser beam seals off the smaller blood vessels, so there is little loss of blood.

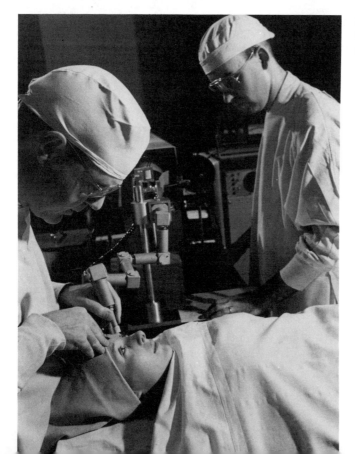

Surgeons use a laser beam for some types of very delicate surgery.

Laser surgery is used mostly on parts of the body where it is difficult or dangerous to use a scalpel—such as the eye, ear, throat, and reproductive systems. It is also used in cutting tissue in parts of the body that have a rich blood supply where there is danger of much bleeding, such as the brain. And certain cancer cells can be destroyed by the heat of a laser as a beam slowly scans an affected area.

Ophthalmologists very often use lasers to treat eye problems. Sometimes the retina pulls away from the wall of the eyeball. Surgeons aim short pulses of intense laser light into the patient's eye. The heat of the beam welds the retina back in place. Before laser surgery, correcting a detached retina was a long and difficult hospital procedure. Today the patient can be treated in the doctor's office and go home afterwards.

Military

Since the 1970s, the armed forces has been using lasers to help aim guns and missiles. Sometimes the laser beam serves as a sort of radar, locating and measuring the distance to an enemy target, and giving this information to an artillery battery. Or, the reflection of the invisible beam guides a tracking missile to a direct hit.

More recently the military has put lasers to work as actual weapons. A powerful laser light can knock out enemy missiles and satellites that include some sort of sighting device. Such devices usually operate at very low levels of light. The super-intense laser light can overload and "blind" the equipment just as easily as it damages human sight.

The army has also found uses for the great heat that lasers can produce. There are laser weapons to vaporize everything from thick armor to delicate electronic systems inside enemy aircraft, missiles, tanks, and warships. The United States has already used super-high-energy laser heat beams to shoot down dummy missiles and unmanned drone planes. Secret research is now concerned with developing even more powerful lasers.

The soldier uses a portable laser to spot an enemy target and direct fire to destroy it.

Military lasers already come in many sizes and shapes. Some are operated by soldiers in the field. Others are located in high-flying airplanes. And it is believed that a number are in satellites circling the earth at a height of 22,000 miles. Although the laser is not yet the "death ray" of science fiction, it is still a powerful modern weapon.

The American military is also now researching defense systems that will protect against lasers. One approach is to cover targets with reflective material that will bounce back the laser rays. Another is to protect the target by blanketing it with many thin layers of material so that each one absorbs some of the laser's energy. A different approach is to have the surface layer of the target spinning around very fast. This lessens the laser impact by spreading it out over a larger area.

Future military preparedness involves the use of lasers too. In the mid 1980s, President Ronald Reagan launched a huge military research program called SDI, from Strategic Defense Initiative. Dubbed "Star Wars" after the futuristic movie of that name, SDI aims to set up a defensive system of lasers and advanced computers. The stated purpose is to destroy enemy missiles and warheads before they strike American targets.

Industry

Lasers are already at work in many factories. They do many things—from drilling holes in everything from diamonds to steel plates to cutting out patterns for metal airplane bodies and men's cloth suits.

A diamond is the hardest natural material. It used to take a worker two days to pierce a diamond by hand. Today the gem can be cut in minutes with a few blasts from a high-energy laser. When the heat of a laser beam is concentrated to a tiny point, it can produce temperatures higher than 10,000° Farenheit—hot enough to drill a hole right through a diamond.

A variety of hard metals, even in thick sheets, are being cut by lasers. Often a jet of pure oxygen is blown at the target of the laser beam. The oxygen reacts with the hot metal and burns it away along the cut. The laser/ oxygen slit is usually narrower than that made with a metal saw.

But laser energy is also good for making holes in soft materials. Since the laser does not actually touch or bend the material, it is much more accurate than mechanical drills. CO_2 lasers often make the pin-sized openings in baby-bottle nipples and spray-can nozzles, as well as the microscopic holes in cigarette paper and drug capsules.

Other soft materials, such as rubber, plastic and cloth fabrics, are starting to be snipped by lasers. In the case of woven plastic seat belts, the laser beam seals the ends as it cuts and thereby prevents unraveling.

A laser is better than almost anything else for welding, or joining together, two pieces of metal. Welding requires only a low-energy laser. Either solid (ruby or YAG) or gas (CO_2) lasers are used to unite pieces of metal up to two inches thick. They can even connect wires that are sealed inside a glass tube.

One of the early uses of lasers in industry was to cut the cloth patterns for men's suits.

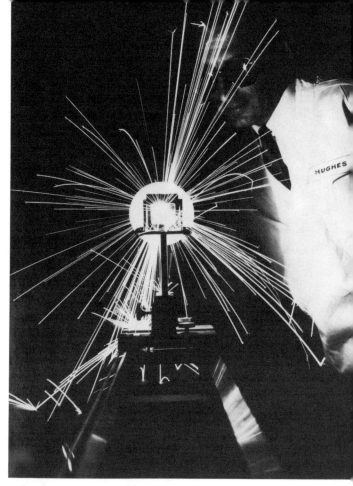

A laser sets off a display of fireworks as it cuts through a sheet of metal.

Measurement

How would you measure the distance across the Grand Canyon? Not an easy task. Someone once said it would take 100 surveyors an entire year to do it right. Yet, recently, two surveyors using lasers made all the measurements in just three days.

Basically their method was quite simple. They set up a laser on one side of the canyon and a mirror on the opposite side. Then they sent a short pulse of laser light to the mirror, which reflected it straight back. A photodetector on the laser measured the time it took for the pulse to make the round trip. Since they already knew the speed of light, they were then able to calculate the exact distance from point to point. By moving the laser/mirror system along the length of the canyon, they were quickly able to complete the task.

Lasers are extremely handy for making exact smaller measurements as well. Take a factory that makes automobile engine blocks, for instance. The front end of the block has to be exactly flat. As the block moves down the assembly line, a beam of a laser light strikes the engine-block end. If the light is reflected straight back to a photodetector, the front is flat. If the light goes off at an angle and does not reach the receiver, the block is crooked and has to be adjusted.

Now imagine an automatic bakery where each loaf of bread has to be at least 4 inches tall. A laser is beamed across the conveyor belt at a height just under four inches. If the light passes over a loaf of bread that is too short and strikes a photodetector on the other side of the conveyor, an alarm warns the baker that a loaf did not rise high enough. If the light is blocked, the bread is the correct height.

Nuclear Fusion

Nuclear fusion is the most awesome source of power and energy known today. It is, as you know from chapter 1, the result of the joining of atoms of hydrogen to create atoms of helium. The heat and light energy of the sun come from the continuous nuclear fusion going on in its interior. Likewise, the superpowerful hydrogen, or H-bomb, gets its amazing force from nuclear fusion.

For decades researchers have been trying to control the nuclear fusion reaction to provide a practical source of energy on earth. But scientists have been unable to reach the millions of degrees of temperature needed to start the reaction. Nor have they been able to create a container in which to hold the superhot hydrogen gas.

One of the most promising approaches to controlled nuclear fusion depends on the laser. The center of laser-fusion research is at the Lawrence Livermore National Laboratory in Livermore, California. Scientists here have

Nova's divided beam is amplified in the long tubes before being sent to the target chamber.

The ten beams of Nova all converge on a tiny pellet inside the huge chamber to create the fusion energy.

built one of the most powerful lasers in the world. This laser, called Nova, can deliver up to 100 trillion watts of power!

The scientists divide a single laser beam into 10 separate beams and send them through 460-foot-long tubes where they are further amplified. All ten beams are aimed at a 16-foot-wide aluminum chamber. At the center of the chamber is a tiny pellet (about the size of a grain of sand) which contains the hydrogen. The beams zap the little speck for a small fraction of a second to bring it up to nearly 5,000,000° Farenheit. At this temperature the hydrogen atoms fuse, sending out a burst of fusion energy.

The results are helping experts learn how to use laser-fusion as an efficient energy source. Some experimenters now say that nuclear fusion will be a practical reality by the 21st century.

Reading

Of all laser uses, perhaps the most common is as a label reader at supermarket checkout counters. Have you ever bought something like a can of soup at a supermarket? Did the checkout clerk slide the can over an opening in the counter? And did you hear a beep and see the price appear on a small screen over the cash register?

At the heart of the automatic checkout is a low-power HeNe laser with a red beam. The HeNe laser is used because there is no need for greater intensity. Also the weaker beam protects people from possible eye damage.

The clerk passes the item over the opening in the counter with the printed stripes of the UPC (Universal Product Code) facing down. Coded in those stripes is the name of the manufacturer (let's say, Campbell Soup Company) and a description of the product (tomato soup), its weight (10¾ oz.) and its price.

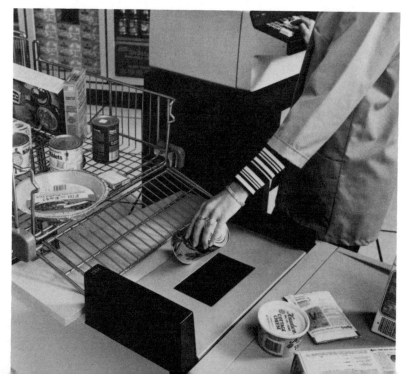

A laser hidden inside the counter reads the zebra-like lines on each product.

The laser beam bounces off the UPC and strikes a photodetector set within the counter. The receiver causes the beeper to sound. It also signals a computer. The computer memory finds the price, shows it on the screen, and prints it on the paper tape that becomes your receipt.

Lasers also read printed or even written words and letters. The system is called OCR, short for Optical Character Recognition. The laser beam scans the text. The reflected light is sensed by a photodetector connected to a computer. The computer then matches the reflected light to a letter shape stored in its memory. The letters are assembled into words and can be used in any number of ways. The computer can "say" the words out loud, it can set type to print the text, or it can enter the words in its memory for some other purpose.

Compact Discs

Until the 1980s, sound could be permanently recorded in only two ways. One was as wiggly grooves on a flat, round phonograph disc. The other was as a pattern of tiny magnetized metal particles on a long, narrow length of tape.

But in 1983 a completely new recording method was introduced, based on the development of lasers and other technologies. Sound could now be recorded as microscopic spots and pits arranged in a spiral on a small, flat disc. Such a recording is called a CD, or compact disc.

The CD is played on a special phonograph. A semiconductor laser beam shines up on the CD from below. A photodetector, also under the CD, senses the difference between light reflected from a flat spot and light reflected from a pit. The phonograph then changes this pattern back into sound, and the listener hears the music.

CDs are better than most conventional records and tapes. They produce more realistic sound than other methods. The record can hold up to 75 minutes of uninterrupted music, much more than the usual record or tape.

The heart of a compact disc player is a laser beam shining up at spots and pits on the disc.

And since the disc has a protective plastic coating and nothing touches the surface, the CDs can last forever.

Holography

In 1947 Dr. Dennis Gabor, a Hungarian scientist working in England, was trying to improve the electron microscope by creating three-dimensional (3-D) images. His idea was to divide the light from a single source into two beams. One, called the *object beam,* he would bounce off the object and onto a photographic plate. The other, called the *reference beam,* he would aim at a mirror, which would reflect the beam onto the same photographic plate.

When the two light waves reached the photographic plate, the waves would bump into, or *interfere* with, each other. They would create an interference pattern. Where the two waves arrived in phase—crest to crest, trough to trough—they would reinforce each other and create a light area on the film. Where they were out of phase—crest to trough, trough to crest—they would cancel each other out and there would be darkness. The image then would not be of the object itself but of the interference pattern of the two beams of light.

According to Dr. Gabor's theory, though, if light was then passed through the developed photographic plate, something strange would happen. The image would appear in 3-D! If the viewers moved their heads up or down or from side to side its appearance would change, just as it does when looking at a solid object.

Gabor called this new approach holography from the Greek words *holos* (meaning "whole") and *graphos* (meaning "picture"). But he could not actually make a hologram. In order to work, holography required coherent light, and there was no source of coherent light in 1947.

With the invention of the laser (and coherent light) in the early 1960s, holography became a practical possibility. Two American scientists at the University of Michigan, Emmett Leith and Juris Upatnieks, showed how to use lasers to create holograms.

Here is the arrangement Leith and Upatnieks devised. They aim a laser beam at a partially silvered mirror, called a *beam-splitter* mirror. The beam-splitter allows some light, the object beam, to pass straight through. This beam is reflected by another ordinary mirror and goes through a lens that spreads out the beam to illuminate the object. Say that the object is a vase of flowers. In this case the light is reflected from the flowers onto the photographic plate.

Another part of the original laser beam, the reference beam, is sent off at an angle by the beam-splitter mirror. It is then reflected by another mirror and passes through a spreading lens that focuses it directly onto the photographic plate.

On the plate the laser light waves of the object and reference beams create an interference pattern of dark and light. And it is this pattern—not a picture of the flowers—that is recorded on the plate. The photographic plate is then developed, and the 3-D image can be seen by shining a laser beam through the developed plate. Or a print can be made from the plate. Then, if the print is illuminated by the laser beam, it gives the same 3-D effect.

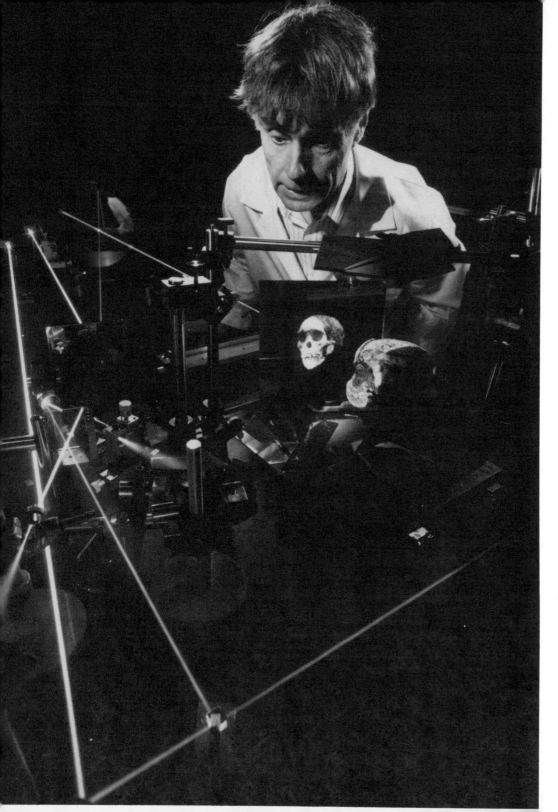

A special holography table is used to make a hologram of a skull that is over one million years old.

The hologram of the fossil skull as it appeared on the cover of a magazine.

Holograms are highly realistic. Many people reach out and try to touch the 3-D object that they see in space. But there is nothing there. The hologram is just a wonderful illusion.

Recently, a way has been found to view laser-created holograms in ordinary light. When you move your head from side to side, you actually see the image in 3-D. But when you move your head up and down, you see only a rainbow spectrum of colors. Such holograms have already appeared on magazine covers and book jackets. Many credit cards now also have these ordinary-light holograms. They are made of thin sheets of aluminum-coated plastic with very fine ridges built in. It is these ridges that allow you to see the changing images of the hologram.

The science of light has made remarkable advances from the primitive candles and oil lamps to the advanced lasers found in today's modern laboratories. And the future is indeed "bright" as scientists learn ever more about lights, lenses and lasers.

Glossary

Absorbed light   The light that is taken in, or not reflected, by a surface.

Analog format   A way of sending information through a glass fiber by varying the brightness of the light wave.

Arc lights   Powerful sources of illumination, such as spotlights or searchlights.

Artificial light   The light from electric light lamps or other man-made sources of light.

Bioluminescence   Biological light produced without heat, such as the light of fireflies.

Candela   A standard of light intensity, based on the light given off by the metal platinum when it is heated until it glows.

CD   Compact disc; a new way of making records based on lasers.

Coherent light   Light in which the waves stick together over a long period of time. Lasers produce coherent light.

Concave lens   A lens that is thin in the middle and thick at the edges; one that spreads out the rays of light that pass through.

Converge   Lines that tend to meet in a point.

Convex lens   A lens that is thick in the middle and thin at the edges; one that brings together rays of light that pass through.

Diaphragm   A device for controlling the amount of light entering a camera, microscope, etc.

Digital format   A way of sending information through a glass fiber by translating the information into a pattern of very short, rapid on-off bursts of laser light.

Diverging rays   Rays of light that spread out, making objects appear smaller than they really are.

Double concave lens   A lens that is pinched in on both front and back.

Double convex lens   A lens that is curved out on both sides like the outside of a circle or sphere.

Eyepiece lens   The lens nearest to the eye of the viewer in a telescope, microscope, etc.

Fiber optics   The transmission of images by bundles of fine, transparent fibers.

Filament   A length of very thin tungsten wire through which electricity flows inside an electric lamp.

Focal length   The distance from the focus to the center of the lens.

Focus   The point at which light rays come together.

Footcandle   A unit of light equal to the amount of light cast by 1 candle at a distance of 1 foot; equal to 1 lumen per square foot.

Fusion   A thermonuclear reaction in which nuclei of certain atoms join to form nuclei of heavier atoms; also called nuclear fusion.

Hologram   An approach to making three-dimensional images based on the laser.

Hue   The quality or shade of color, such as red, blue, etc.

Illumination   The amount of light on a surface, such as a book, table or road.

Laser   Acronym of Light Amplification by Stimulated Emission of Radiation.

LCD   Liquid Crystal Display. A source of light on many digital watches and calculators that shows the numbers as black lines against a gray background.

LED   Light-Emitting Diode. The familiar red lights on many stereos, radios, TVs and other electronic equipment that comes from current flow between two attached layers of crystal material.

Lenses   Curved pieces of transparent material, such as glass or clear plastic, that bend the rays of light passing through them.

Light   A form of energy that makes things visible.

Light-year   The distance that light, moving at 186,000 miles per second, travels in one year; about 6 trillion miles.

Lumen   The unit of visible light given off by an electric lamp.

Magnifying power   The ability to make something appear larger than the real size; also called magnification.

Microscope   An instrument with one or more lenses for making small things look larger.

Mirror   Flat pieces of glass covered on one side with a thin layer of silver or other shiny metal.

Monochromatic   Light of only one wave length.

Natural light   Light from the sun.

Objective lens   The lens nearest to what is viewed through a telescope, microscope, etc.

Opaque   Objects that allow no light to pass through them, such as metal, wood, heavy cloth, rocks, etc.

Ophthalmologist   A medical doctor who deals with the structure, functions and diseases of the eye.

Optician   The maker or seller of eyeglasses.

Optometrist   A person trained to examine the eyes and prescribe glasses.

Plano-concave lens   A lens that is flat on one side and concave on the other.

Plano-convex lens   A lens that is flat on one side and convex on the other.

Photons Units of electromagnetic energy.

Prism A wedge of clear glass that separates white light passing through it into the colors of the rainbow.

Quantum theory The concept that light is given off in tiny bundles of energy instead of a steady stream.

Radiant energy A form of energy that spreads out and does work, such as the light from the sun.

Radiate The moving out of light in all directions from its source.

Radio telescope A huge antenna that gathers radio waves from space and brings them to a focus.

Rainbow Created when something splits white light into its basic colors: red, orange, yellow, green, blue, indigo and violet.

Reflected light Light that makes things visible by striking the object and throwing the light back to your eyes.

Reflecting telescope A telescope that uses mirrors to reflect light from the stars and bring it to a focus.

Refracted light Light rays that are bent by the medium through which they pass.

Refracting telescope A telescope that uses glass lenses to bring rays of light to a focus.

Spectrum A band of colors formed when a beam of light is broken up by being passed through some material, such as a prism.

Telescope An instrument for making distant objects appear nearer and larger.

Translucent Objects that allow some light to pass through but not enough to show clear details, such as frosted glass, clouds, thin sheets of paper, some kinds of plastic, etc.

Transparent Objects that let light pass through easily with little or no interference, such as air, clear glass, etc.

Value The darkness or lightness of a color. Also called brightness.

Index